*Dedicated to all my friends
Past,
Present
and Future*

until the right one comes along

chriS haleY

Cupid's Advice

Why do you keep writing love songs?
Why do you still obsess
On the yes and nos
Of romantic woes
Stemmed from hearts that cause the mess?

I tell you
Stop your sweating
Easy come, easy go is the way
There are a billion people
Running around this earth,
Yet, you cry over one lost yesterday?

People get a clue
It's a game
The Matrix plugged you in
If it's not Trinity on Neo
It's the exes and 'yos
That'll start these dramas again.

What I'm trying to say People
Is stop worrying!
Whether the world blows tomorrow
Next week, or a zillion and eight
You will always find love for better or worse

It is your blessing and it is your curse.
The only thing unknown,
Like my arrows when windblown,
Is that for Love,
You can't rehearse.

Perfect Love

There was a mansion, high on a hill
It was so impressive I remember it still
The doors were massive
The windows were gilded bronze
The lawn was immaculate
A pristine landscape I could not tread upon.

In the distance
The house seemed a dream
A masterpiece worth painting
But seldom seen
And in the majestic sunset
As this manor faded from my view
I called it, *Perfect Love,*
For the reality I sought
And also, never knew.

Little Victories

Life is a struggle
Often hard to do
Commit yourself to little victories
And you just might make it through

Living alone

Nothing is sexier than
living alone

Your dreams
welcome you home

Your imagination
dines with you

Your visions
entertain you

Your fantasies
ravage you

Your confidence
cradles you and
rocks you to sleep.

Sometimes a storm comes

Sometimes a storm comes
And you hide from the rain
Huddle where it's dry
As if wet
Would cause you pain

Look outside through a beaded window
At dark, full cheeked clouds,
Like they are themselves
The most frightening of sights
As if nature
Bringing nature around you
Is horrid
And terribly not right.

No wonder personalities
Confound you
Your spirit shrinks when met
With the simplest display of
Confusion
Or rejection
From an unknown gent.

As storms come and go

Appreciate the strength they direct
Admire yourself for facing them
And surviving
With your soul's pure intent
To find one to lead you
Through the dark clouds
Break them with the umbrella
Of the bright sunlight
The warmth you can only feel
The heat you can only get
From another who loves you dearly
Inside and outside
Dry or wet.

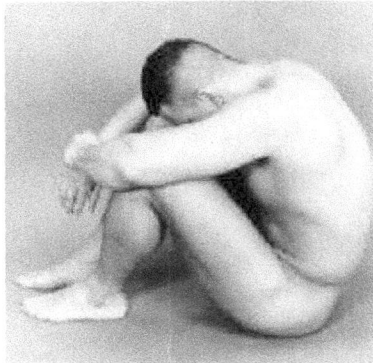

Dry Night

Stopped in
Sauntered by
Walked fast
Winked an eye.
Stared past the strobe
Looking for a worthy "Hi."
Saw none
Gazed down
Next week
Another try.

laughing

I go in
And I want to start laughing.
The pretentiousness of
So many on the floor
Posing, primping, scoping,
Making one guy's eye contact
Avoiding another's
I want to bend over, double,
And howl.

But I am here alone and
I would look stupid.
Then no one would try
My eye contact
Or pose, primp, and scope me.

I would still have no one
To laugh with.

I had a hunk
I couldn't fuck
I had a hand
Which couldn't wake me
I had my eyes
That couldn't believe
This failure would overtake me

I had this guy
Whose body was *bomb*
And my pacifist dick said
"Whoa."

So when I finally achieved
My own attention
Stuffed the boy suitably tight
He exploded long and high
On my chest, abs, and thigh.
Then slipped up and off
Smiling into the night
Leaving me full and wet
To fret, jack, and shout.
"Impotent, impotent,
Not the way to be
When lying beneath you
Is a twitching bubble butt booty."

It's true what they sang in Hair

White boys with rhythm
Drive me crazy.
My stomach stirs when they move
I want to eat them up.
No matter their face and form
They rate at least a 7
When they can shake
That Caucasian rump.

I want to capture
One
Of these frisky toys
Hold him close
Wrap my arms
Around his bobbing back,
Circling hands,
Pulsing hips,
Scuttling feet,
Squeeze him against my body
So all our sweat glands meet
But loose enough
That he can wiggle
And the air can share our heat.

My system absorbs his being
My eyes glaze
My flesh burns
My legs tremble
My loin busts
Aahhhhh
I slowly let him
Slide
Free.

Let me catch just one
Vanilla-toned
Dancing man.

I Wonder

He jumped and gyrated
Flailed his arms and shook.
Eyes closed and it seemed
Conscious only of the music
And himself.
He appeared at the end of the night
Too late for a plot, a ploy,
To cook.

I wondered.
I wondered.

I watched him leave
And I wondered.

Does it matter when someone stands
Next to you
Then jiggles and wiggles and prances about
Is it a sign
They want to be ~ with

Or only that
They like to dance.

Sunday Evening

Mmmmmm
Russian man
Sexy Black
Deep lidded eyes of the one
Steady, deadly stride of the other
Two considerations
Interesting
And worth a second glance...

But on the unusual occasion
Of a Sunday evening
Neither perfect enough
To warrant a chance.

100,000 Songs

What are the ways?
What are the ways?
What are the ways?

What are the ways
To be happy

What are the ways
To be gay

What are the ways
To be in love
For a hundred thousand days?

What are the things
You have to say
To make sure
He doesn't go away?
What are the ways
To be happy
For a hundred thousand days?

What are the decisions
You should make,

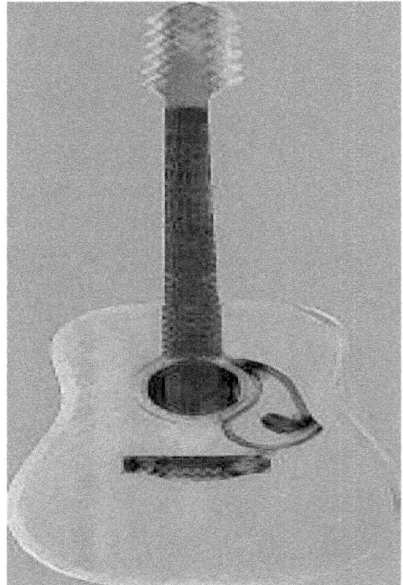

The offers you should take,
The compliments you should say
The others you should shake?

Which shy smile
Makes him cling
While the other makes him shy away
What are the moves that
Push you closer to
A hundred thousand days?

I've had a day,
Here and there,
When everything was right.
I smelled love on the horizon,
My heart raced at his sight.
But
Not many are smitten as easily
They know these 'things'
Come and go
For me they leave so often
I strive to hold them so...

I smile too broad
I wink too soon
I touch too softly
I openly swoon

I stare too long
And then I'm left lonely
Having done nothing wrong
Yet, again I've hatched new lyrics
For a theme born one hundred thousand times
Someone single, unhappy;
Song 100,009.

Tell me what you will

Tell me something good
Speak to me words of joy
Whisper in my direction
Encouragement
Convince me I'm
The luckiest of boys,

Tell me something good
Make me believe its true
And say it not because
I asked you
But because the notice was
Long overdue.

Tell me
Please tell me
Something good.

What I Want

I want somebody

To hold me
When I'm crying,
To hug me,
When I'm down,
And say
Without my asking,
"Honey,
Everything's
Gonna be all right."

A Sad Romantic View

Hate
Isn't so bad
It means
I affect you.

Love
Is only a chance
At wonderful
For it can one day
Fade
To like.

Indifference
Is the worst
It shows
I've touched you not.
Indifference
Is the worst feeling
That I have ever got.

If I had an alternative

**And now
I am a sinner.**

**Or so a friend
Declares me to be.
He is born again.
I am gay.
"Condemned", he says to me.**

**The second time
The second time
This friend has refused my being,
But softer and gentler now
More humane
Than the first
At one with Christ
And the Bible,
He can not be
At peace with me.
Phone calls are all right...
If I am in need
Stalled on the side of the road He
is allowed to help**

But socialize, no.
Condone it, no.
Or he
Would be a sinner, too.

Today, the church allows him
Charity
The kindness I have shown him
He can show me
To a degree
Before
He was set to cast me aside
Completely
Before his new found Christianity.
Yesterday, the church agreed
That he show me none.
Today
There is a window
No, perhaps a fence
He may speak to me through
From behind which he can
Touch me
Thus the Holy view
Will not seem
Too Unholy.

I tell my friend

My friend of eleven years
That I believe in God, too,
The God who made me Gay
Who made him straight
The same way.
From man and woman.
Should I believe
He made me a sinner?
An abomination against Himself.

Why?
A test?
I struggled through years
Of self-denial
Recrimination
Regret
Fear
Disillusion
Refusing to accept myself
But never hate
Because somewhere deep
Deep deep inside
I thought He decided this
Somehow it must be right.
Still I was chaste
Celebate because of my insecurity
Shy of both sexes

Seeking a positive sign
Emotion, desire,
Opportunity to explore uninhibited lust
Then I might know
All through this abnormal
Unnatural time
Of stunted sexual growth
I was good
As good as I could be
If being with no one was good
My respect for truth
For pure honesty
That kept me lonely
Led me to that day
When I admitted to myself
It would be a lie
It would be a sin
To take a woman
When I had been born
To desire a man.

If Gay is wrong
If God created this test for me
And millions of others
Since time began
Then time again
Will let me realize this

Not the threats or condemnations
Of scared, closed minded others.
And time will bless my soul with acceptance.

To allow mortal pressure
To force me to 'change',
After the agony of years of denial
After embracing a courage of self acceptance
I fear a religiously dictated reversal
Would clap me in a tower again
A tower of my own secret shame
That I was ever this 'thing'

I will not lie
I will not rescind
I asked
I begged
I cried
"God, why have you given me this pain?"
But is the pain overcoming being Gay
Or struggling to accept it?
What I will demand of my God
What I will give myself
Is the right to respect
My own honesty.
I believe truth
Is what he would want me to be.

COMMUNION

I was stunned
When I looked into his eyes
While he stood on the altar steps,
And his smile spread angelic and sweet.
I focused on the size
Of his frame, of his torso,
Of the shoes on his feet.
I thought his lips too thin,
But then our gazes met.
He wore civilian clothes,
A flowered tan rayon shirt.
I'd seen him here often before
But I saw him at a club once
And it made my face jerk.
So here I was considering,
As the new pastor spoke
Homophobic prose,
Could this lay minister be
Hiding the same as me.
I raised my eyes
And forced myself
To stare at him.
He struck me as adorably cute.

I lost myself in this moment.
All sound was muted.
Everyone else had cupped their palms
To accept the wafer of life.
I opened my mouth
And offered my hands.
I felt right in both efforts
But I left him befuddled,
Unsure of what to do;
Go first to my tongue,
Then to my hands.
I withdrew them.
Into my mouth he knew
To place the bread
And I withdrew.
After "The Body of Christ"
He said "I'm sorry."
My manner had caused such confusion.
I said "That's all right."
And retreated to my pew
Touched, curious, and wondering
If any deeper connection
Had accompanied that communal food.

Home For a Change

Late in the evening
And you went nowhere
Reluctant to appear in
Your favorite lair
Afraid of rejection
Wanting to miss those you've seen
Wishing there was another place hipper
Where the boys are also clean
Cut and preppy looking
Reminiscent of all you'd want
For a frivolous night of boffing
Whether it led to love or not.

The Way

When crying is the constant action you nurture
When smiling is the game you falsely play
When living is the dynamic you question daily
When dormant sleep is the only peace that passes your way

You need to find a fresh horizon
Quickly, you must dig a new pathway
Urgently, you should grab a rope that's dangling
And swing yourself to a landing that escapes yesterdays.

When everyone follows you and yet
You're lonely
When your full schedule leaves you empty
Every hectic day
It is time to cut back on evasive activities
And embrace a calming search for serenity

Poetic Days

The day is past
I sit at last to
Write a verse with yet
No class
Hoping to release some
Positive vibe
To create an upswing from
A downswing time

Escape the pessimism of
Ventures unfulfilled but
Packed with dreams
Begging to be willed
In spite of innumerable nos
And maybes
And I don't have the time
People whose excuses are so paltry
That inside I laugh
At every line
At every smirk

How folk can believe it's better
To drift along on another's rope
Than build their own twine
Laced with purpose and hope

Are we all so soft to ever
Avoid the struggle and
Postpone the journey
It takes to succeed
How long have I
Been so weak
Accepted what I got, not
What I deserve and need.

Fuck that I won't give up
People can whine their lives away
I won't bemoan my challenging path
My heart will beat proudly every day.

Cards

I don't know how
To play Texas Hold'em
I don't have a clue
About 5 Card Stud
Two Aces beat Two Kings
I've been told
But Poker
I'm still a dud.

I want to go to Vegas though
To play the game of Hearts
Joker, Queen, or Deuces Wild.
I only ask to play a part.
Don't care the order
Don't care the bet
Just let me play
I will win, yet.

alternative

Why does she wave
When she leaves my sight
Why do our eyes light
When they meet
Why do we voluntarily wait
For the other
When its time to leave or eat
Why this if she likes another
Why this
If romance is not meant to be
Why tease me with a
Female attraction
If I am meant for
Male comradery

Does this test
Lead to a final answer
Or questions broader still
Are you saying my life is yet
Open to decide
Or am I solely
A game at Your will.

Albany

And so it has happened
On one midtemp night
That my cruising
From one bar to another
Gained me a pleasing sight.

Cute, sweet, gentle
An Albany man I spied
For moments...
We shared wallflower glances
Then my choosiness
Chose to subside.

As nice as any here I've encountered
As genuine as any I've
Briefly known
He assures me its friendship he's after
Yet,
He's the nearest to surpass that
I've been shown.

As summer rages on
The temperatures get hotter
The cool nights reveal

A bright moon,
I'll hum to myself
I've found another
At last, perhaps,
I can swoon

hold your hand to my heart

Hold your hand to my heart
And feel it beating
Sense my blood running through
To touch your fingertips
Read my eyes
Begging you to linger
And my lips
Praying that you'll stay

Hold your hand to my heart
Sense our skin adhese
My pores sweat glue to
Hold you fast
Smile politely
Sweetly say
It can't be this way.

Hold your hand to my heart
Kiss and embrace me
With warm breath whisper
Your ex and you are one again

In 25 days you'll leave
You'll rejoin him
Hug me tight
As disappointment melts my soul

Hold your hand to my heart
Say goodbye
Comfort me with wide eyes
Seeing my regret
And knowing
There's nothing left to say.

Hold your hand to my heart
Don't pull it away
Don't go
Don't go
But if you must
Shield my sight
Mute my senses

I'll only remember
When you stood there
Holding your hand to my heart this way.

Arizona Angel

Arizona Angel Gabriel
Were you really all that sweet?
Or is the thirst for attention so intoxicating
Your standing next to me made my heart skip beats

On a scale of 1 to 10
You were probably a 6 or 7
Your smile and spirit might
Raise you to a situational 8
Yet for the moment, for the moments
I was considering you
Gabriel from Arizona
And Chris from DC did relate

Then the creepy man separated us
Simultaneously your friends happened by
Off in their company you wandered
As if we in our passing
Had never passed by

Arizona Angel Gabriel
Were you really all that sweet?
When you stood across the room
And suddenly appeared next to me
Was it coincidence or

Did you actually want to meet?

Blow your horn Gabriel
Tune your music slow
I hope you find life happy and
A loving man
I'll keep looking for my gift from Heaven
A physically angelic figure who'll stay
Where I stand.

sympatico

I laugh because
I am fine
And it does me no good
I laugh because
Per the cliche of it
My friends are convinced it should.

I squint because
I'm told
I'm placed high on the wanted list
I cry because
Apparently
That's easy to resist

If I am so
Good looking
If I am so
Damn fine
Why am I
Still looking
Why doesn't someone rule my time?

Someone sneak me the answer
Someone grind me the key

I've sauntered to a zillion doors
And seldom been invited
Where I didn't want to leave.

I want a long-term relationship
I've had my one-night stands
I want something secure and lasting
I want a sympatico man.

Look Out of Your Mind's Eye

Look out of your mind's eye
Dig deep in to the tunnel of your being
Reach out from your soul through your vision
And grasp the wonder of others
Looking out their mind's eye at you

Shallow

Could I write a poem about
The folks I turned away
Admit to the bitching I dished and pitched
Like Dynasty and Dallas
Sweet mellow me
Both night and day,
The abrupt lack of concern and false confirmations
Brought to true deceit in light
How many have I dissed and
Forgotten they crossed my way
Remembering only those who didn't
Give my ego sway
 Can I admit to my shallow indulgences that
Tore the hearts of those who
Might well say
He was a simple playa
Teased me and then strutted away
Just like all the other cute guys who wink
Tease, laugh, and clear the path
Dangling a tasty phone number
Never to be sampled just thrown away
Wasting and tearing feelings
By sharing contacts of those you

Discard through forced memories
So all you acknowledge is
The hurt you claim you've endured all alone
And such the pure person for struggling so.

Meeting a Dreamboat at the door

Wow

"$5 dollar cover..."

Will you hold me close
And love me
Will you love me
If I let you hold me close

Will you kiss me with
Tenderness
When I'm frightened;
Caress me with your arms
When I'm unsure
Protect me
When I'm defenseless and
When I'm sick
Be my cure

Will you accept my rapt embraces
Receive the advances I throw
Relish the attention
I lavish on you

Before everyone we do
And do not know

Will you love me
As I'll love you
Forever
Or should we end this now
And let it go?

"...Thanks.
Have a nice night."
My lips drew in his fragance
As he turned
And faded into the crowd

Maybe
When he returns for his coat...

It's a quarter to three

Bartender
My eye bender
Gorgeous, young, lean one
How often I watched you pour
Followed your walk
Your long stalk
Up and down the bar rail
Searching for another glass to fill

I have hunted your deep brown eyes
And probed them for a tantalizing sign
That you notice me
That you wonder about me
That you want me
Seeking to receive the same message
My eyes have been sending you
For an interminably long, mysterious, time.

How many hundreds have ogled you
In the three years I've adored you from afar
How many have you kindly turned away
How many have you amorously encouraged to stay
How many have you longed for
But they got away

In which group might I fall
If I began to pursue you day after day.

Will I ever find a way to decode
Your stoic stare,
That kind
But not too friendly gaze
Calmly accepting my tip,
Into a wish that
I'd offer you more?

Only time will tell
And I'll keep it well
Hello, Joe!
How about another one
Because you close the doors?

Queasy

I see you
I go queasy
It's embarrassing
But it's true
The sight of you in my presence and
My senses melt to goo

The compliments I feel inside me
Which mirror the thoughts I think of you
Stumble through my lips
Tripped by nerves and indecision
Each time I try a few

Even now
After we've spoken
You know a little about me
I know a morsel about you
I stutter at new conversation
Which might reveal a future
In my rapt pursuit of you

I realize it's not love
I know I don't know you that well
But it's amazing how this

Infatuation
Makes me ponder you so deeply
Like I might a lover of several years

It's only "Hi."
"How are you?"
"How's it going tonight?"
"Nothing new."
"Make any money?"
"You're so cute."
"You're sweet."

And enduring the anxiety which
Lets me go no further
So all I do
Is write about you
Convince myself
That these small exchanges
Somehow
Mean more.

But isn't it great to know
If you know
That you make someone
Queasy.

I dreamt of you last night

I dreamt of you last night
And it was sweet
Like one of those movie scenes
We talked real deep
We spoke real low
Then our eyes grew hazy
And our lips said hello

We held each other close
You asked me if
I wanted to go home
I said "Yes." with a slight whimper
My legs were numb
My heart was beating so

We got to your apartment
We lay in your bed
We languised for a moment
Feeling the dimensions of our manhood spread

And then slowly
But suddenly
We were like a couple and
You had to go

I understood because
I Knew you'd be back
After all
We loved each other so.

Then the worst thing
That can happen
In a dream
Instantly did
I woke up in my lonesome reality
And remembered the horrible dread
You weren't mine
We hadn't kissed on the lips
We hadn't swallowed each others' tongues
We hadn't caressed each others' hips

Because I had been a heartbeat
From asking you out the night before
And inexplicably, choked,
When after I asked you
If you had a boyfriend
You said "No."

I took you home
In my fantasy
Where you were my boyfriend for a night

Though that wasn't enough even
In my dreams

Now I'm awake
And I wish it was always night.

BEAUTIFUL MIRROR

I walked by a mirror
In a local department store
I caught a glimpse
A reflection
Of someone who looked
Interesting
Who looked
Maybe
Beautiful
I took an overt glance
A more obvious stare
And I almost laughed until I cried
I almost laughed until I died
I almost laughed
I almost
I
Didn't
Because
That beautiful vision
Was me
And for so many years
I had thought
I was not much to look at
Not much to glance
Or stare at
And there I was
Momentarily intrigued
By me

How different my life might have been
Might be
If I had thought this
Believed this
Years and years ago
In my impressionable
Spongelike youth
How much stronger I might have been
Might be
But no
As this beautiful image
In a mirror
Reflected
Only recently
Have I come to appreciate
Me
And because of this
I almost laughed
Until I cried
And died
Almost
Almost
But the beautiful mirror
Also showed me
That I've survived.

A Poem 4 Abass

When you smile the world glows
And I am frightened to be in its light
Scared you will see the beat of my heart
The blood rushing to where my lips loose control

That your beam will read how you affect me
That you are why my words mumble, stumble and fail
That only with time can my tongue regain control
Only with time could my heart express emotions to sail

Us through all obstacles
Grab the wings of eagles and soar to heights above high
Envelop you with arms that would protect you forever
Cover you with love that would warm you through all time

But now my every motion, emotion is halted
Stunned and immobilized by the gleam of your face
So captivated by the vision of your expression
That none of my dreams have the breath to leave

My inner place that wants you
The soul that prays to kneel in your grace
The arms, the legs that fantasize of waking in your web
The eyes that long to grow tired and old
Staring into the smile
That makes the world glow

Ash Blonde

I thought of you
The other day
It was cloudy, cold, and hazy
Must be why my mind
Let you back in
The weather had made me lazy

Riding through miles and miles of fallen trees
I remembered our highs and lows
I recalled the evening we sat
Across a round brown table and said "Hi"
And the blue ink on yellow paper
In the letter where you wrote "Let go"

I curse changing seasons for triggering memories
Running video clips from your past
Mellow moments buried in your heart
That your brain hoped wouldn't last

Second Thoughts

Why do I cry
As I leave you
When it was I who left
So long ago

Why do I smart
At your mention of another
I had wished you no less
When I chose to go.

Why are my months and years
So lonely
When, again, with you
These last days
I felt full.

Why did I leave you
To leave myself lonely
Why was I
Why was I
such a fool?

Too Good For Me

My friend says "Jo"
She doesn't know you
She doesn't know how good you are
But then
I didn't know either
And you were there for me
Easy to see
Unhassled and free
But damaged as I've been
You were too good for me

I'd never known people
Who really liked me
Romantically
Who liked how I looked
How I behaved
How I was
Me
You liked me from the start
Loved me with your heart
Bought me chocolates
Sent me pictures
Worshiped mine
So Sweet, so kind
How could you ever be mine

Thank you so
For showing me love I didn't know

And couldn't hold
I'm so new to feeling worthy
It scares me away
Thank you for showing me
That someone
Could possibly
Care for me
This way
Hopefully
I'll find another who
Loved me like you
And I won't again be the jerk
I've most often known
Who ignores the pearl in his face
For the glass that cracks
And fractures all chances
For loves that last.

My Jo
My Jo
You should've been my Jo
And you were
You could have been
But my heart couldn't sense it
So you knew
And I, too,
That so often in my life
The truly good ones
Have to go.

And sadly I write this
Tears welling in my eyes
What right, how trite
I had him
And I didn't want him
Now I'm back
Where I wanted to be
Unhappy, alone,
Not loving who loved me
And unloved by the one I do
Still fucked up
Still fucked up
What's a grown, lonely man to do?

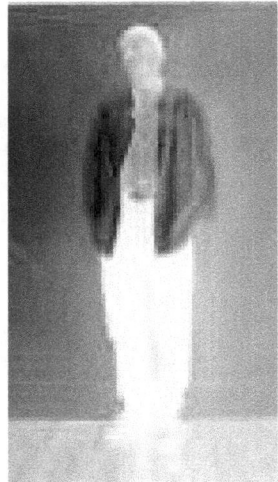

The Moment's Passed

Joyous Heaven comes to me
In the eyes of those staring
Whom I can not see
Optimistic fate presents hope in my path
With the lustful gazes of those whose
Attention I don't grasp
Lustful sighs silently graze my ears
Which now register only vaguely
Numbed by countless muted years

The one from Lebanon who waits near me for tips
But captured by another swiftly before my charming attempt could hit
Currently slipping to and fro
Bar back in the popular, cruise bar
"Close friends" he's called me in introductions to others
Though only seated conversations and
Standing drink exchanges have extended our initial meeting thus far

And I see you working
When I graze the club to sip
Wondering the point of niceties
Since our companionship has all ready clipped
Is there a reason for momentary acknowledgments?
When work is always where we greet
You now connected to another
So casually we can no longer break meat

How then can this *friendship* grow
When stifled it was at the first pass
What progress can come from measured chit chat?
Tonight I struggled in speaking to you
Alas, I feel the moment's passed.

The Night is So Beautiful

The night is so beautiful
I'm numb
I don't know what to do
I wish I had someone to share it wish
I guess I still wish that was you

And I know I could call
You'd come running
Excited to be included in my plans
But your heart would be beating platonic
While mine would wish we held hands.

God, the night is so still
Like it's contemplating its next
Climatic move
No mind could avoid wandering
In such a soft and tender mood.

I feel like something should happen
Anything,
A storm, a wind, a breeze
Something to puncture this serenely calm moment
Should I shout right now to the Trees?

I don't believe my life is this steady!
I don't recognize this bliss as true.
Come on, future mishaps, I'm ready!
Nothing on earth is this smooth.

Does this mean I crave the excitement?
The upside down moments that confuse
Our passion for love and
Our love for passion;
The never ending, always burning fuse?

Perhaps, it's so
I'm stunned by this silence
By this pastoral sky of purple blue
I crave the fireworks of our daily rants
When blood, our heated veins, pulsed through.

But this night I'm so numb
That one day, I know
I will be over the drama
And welcome the glow
The glow you recognize
On a beautiful night.

Baby Doll

also known as

The Suite of Vowels

A

Aaaaaaaaaaay sweet baby
And here I thought we were through
Yet once again we've opened our doors
To dreams we'd closed our eyes to

The warm possibility of Companionship
A friendship which held no bounds for
You, no bounds on company
For me, just bound to you; and I found

Our dissimilar ideas were too limiting
You wanted us locked but somehow free
Able to venture wherever life led us
Though close as two could ever be

Aaaaaaaa sweet baby
That just wasn't for me
Hand in hand, arm in arm
Is what I see
As the cause and effect that
Makes a couple
So nothing's changed

But here we are...
Round three

The Suite of Vowels

E

E-E-E-E-Easy does it!
We've only been back together a week
What ever went wrong the first two times
May just be dozing
We don't want to wake it from its sleep!

Slowly and softly
And tenderly
Carefully
Let's walk this thing out
Allow it to sniff out any new surroundings
Before a stiff wind blows old scents in our snouts.

E-E-E-E-Easy does it!!!
I'm not saying I don't want to be here today!
It just seems unwise to rush past go
Let's savor this new beginning
For at least a little while longer
Then, before you know it,
Bingo
I'll be sold.

The Suite of Vowels

I

I yi yi
I knew it
We were acting too hastily
I knew we were running too fast
Whatever takes months to break apart
Can't be fixed just by pushing the gas

I yi yi
We blew it
And we knew we were an explosive sort
Loving as we were and stubborn as we were
Such a tug of war could always end short

So what do we do now
Say bye again
Resign ourselves to *three-quel's* failed path
Or consider our obstacles that keep emerging
And imagine a union that might last.

The Suite of Vowels

O

O-Oh no
I don't believe it
You did something nice without my request
But I am not going to be fooled by momentary madness
I will not be taken in by desperate largess

I can't deny it touches me
I've been a soft touch since the deer's Mama cashed it in
The smallest of gestures can bowl me over
Strike!
Nine more frames of this and you win.

The Suite of Vowels

U

You drive me crazy with your expectations
I can't be nice without your mind going wild
I do good sometimes because I care about you
Not because I want us walking down the aisle.

You put pressure on me to be perfect
To fill some ideal of how a lover should be
I put no expectations on our future
I just want you to be you and
Allow me to be me

You've reached me like no other
It's undeniable
Why we're so close I can't figure, I agree
But it angers me that whenever I do the slightest thing
You clam up and claim *you're getting free!*

You
You
You drive me crazy, I get headaches, I get fevers, I'm
confused, I'm frustrated, I can't conceive
Why our having little rough patches and my
Worshipping you

Still means we can't take things platonically

But I love you and
I want you and
I need you
A future without you I won't concede
Just let me be your baby doll
On my own terms
And I'll make you happy
I promise
Eternally.

Well I guess I waited too Long

I waited for a change of scene
Waited for the rain to clear
Convinced myself that stormy weather
Was all a part of getting there
Now the rain is over
it's sunshine everyday
and still my outlook's cloudy
I think i lost my way

well i guess i waited too long
i guess i hoped too strong
blinded myself to the reality
you were not where i belonged
Although this patience I don't regret
It will help me as I go on
But most of all is this memory
I guess I waited too long.

I know you're crying deeply
To you it makes no sense
That I felt I could take no more
Of this committed non-commit
You cherished me like no other
And I prized you the same
Saying that you'd die for me

Evoked what dare not speak its name
But that type love wasn't your ideal
You felt I misconstrued
So now I'll take what you've given me
On my road to start anew

well i guess i waited too long
i guess i hoped too strong
blinded myself to the reality
you were not where i belonged
Although this patience I don't regret
It will help me as I go on
But most of all is this memory
I guess I waited too long.

But most of all is this memory
I guess I waited too long

Finale

If I told you
We were over?
If I shared
I thought us through?
Would you gently leave the table
And walk away?
Would you accept it
As grownups do?

If I told you
I enjoyed the journey
The bumps and detours too
Would you glean from that
Good tidings?
Could you calmly respond,
Well, me too?

Or would you fight
A torturous battle?
Blame me, blame us
Blame the powers who
Put us together with strong
But separate goals,
Who sprinkled ointment
In our glue?

Should we agree
These years and months
Taught us lessons?
Might we ponder
We always knew
A relationship as intense as ours
Was destined to split in two.

So
This is the finale
This is the ending
This is the fond adieu
Lets promise one thing
Before we go
That this was it, all of it;
There will be no
Déjà vu.

A Love Affair

The closest friendship
Is like a love affair
With highs and lows
And compromises;
With battles and wars
And fights
That are so bitter
And apologies
That are so sweet

Let our love be
Like a friendship
Then I can stand
The withering blows
And the blistering fire
Knowing well we will hang on
For the orgiastic embraces
And the breathless sighs
That may accompany
The tiniest exchange of a gift

Between two companions
Whose closeness is so intense
Whose connection is so passionate
That their friendship is like
A love affair.

So Many Other Restaurants

The truth is
He doesn't love you
The truth may be
He never will

The reality is
You hate this
As you've hated it before
And want to hurt him
By leaving him
And help yourself
By leaving him, too;
But not just him
But this wanting,
This needing
To pursue the one who
Doesn't want you

There is nothing he can
Write now
Or say
That you would truly believe or
Trust
At this point
You would doubt a claim of love
Or forever
Look behind every door and
Unanswered phone call

You look for the worst and
Here it is
You've received it
He aint your lover,
He's your friend
If the future might change things
Then the future will
But for now,
If friend aint what you want
And that's all that's being served
You shouldn't stay staring at a
Disappointing menu
In an uncomfortable venue
You should pay what you owe
And go
There are so many other restaurants.

Until the Right One Comes Along

Baltimore, Waldorf, Guatemala, Nicaragua
Until the right one comes along
Pudgy, husky, toned, skinny
Until the right one comes along
Shy, aggressive, romantic, horny
Until the right one comes along
Closeted, out, butch, republican
Until the right one comes along
Comely, attractive, sexy, pretty
Until the right one comes along
Straight, hard, subtle, raging
Until the right one comes along
Military, waiter, construction, college
Until the right one comes along
Secure, struggling, seasonal, parental
Until the right one comes along
And rich, flamboyant, successful, model-ific

Still

Until the right one comes along

How long should I keep traveling
How long should I stay on the road?
As long as there's breath in my body
As long as hotties still step to say "Hey"
Until I realize (as Jesse says)

I am somebody
Until the Right one comes my way.

**With Special Thanks
to my friend and editor
Carol Youmans**

**Images courtesy of
Dave Milspaugh
Steve Garrett Jr**

www.ingramcontent.com/pod-product-compliance
Lightning Source LLC
Chambersburg PA
CBHW060345050426
42449CB00011B/2839